Also from GHF Press

*Making the Choice: When Typical School
Doesn't Fit Your Atypical Child*

Forging Paths: Beyond Traditional Schooling

**Look for these Authors
Coming Soon from GHF Press**

Ben Curran and Neil Weatherbee:
Incorporating Technology into Homeschooling

Corin Goodwin and Mika Gustavson:
Gifted Homeschooling and Socialization

Pamela Price:
Balancing Work & Real Life with Homeschooling

If This is a Gift,
Can I Send it Back?
Surviving in the Land of the Gifted and Twice Exceptional

By Jen Merrill

Edited by Sarah J. Wilson

Published by GHF Press
A Division of Gifted Homeschoolers Forum
1257 Siskiyou Blvd. #174
Ashland, OR 97520

ISBN-13: 978-0615648781
ISBN-10: 0615648789

Portions of this book have appeared in altered form in previous publications.

Cover design by Shawn Keehne (skeehne@mac.com).

Dedications

For Tom and the boys. I'd have no stories without you.

And Malbec.

Contents

Acknowledgments

It's awfully difficult to acknowledge everyone who supported me as I started down the book-writing path. For starters, a great majority of them live in my computer; someday, perhaps, we'll actually meet and lift a glass to one another.

Thank you to all the parents of gifted and twice-exceptional parents who have shared their stories and frustrations over the last few years. Your generosity and willingness to share has touched me deeply; know you are far from alone on this journey.

Thank you to Deborah Mersino, founder of #gtchat (found on Twitter), for your support of my writing and starting me down this road. You have no idea what it means to me.

Thank you to Lisa Lauffer, for convincing me that yes, I *am* a gifted adult and that I do have gifts to share. Huh. Who knew?

Thank you to Corin Barsily Goodwin, founder of Gifted Homeschoolers Forum, for your encouragement as I jumped, scared to death, into the adventure of homeschooling a kid smarter than I am.

Thank you to Sarah Wilson, editor extraordinaire, for keeping me in line with the patience of a saint.

Thank you to Christine Fonseca, for living the writer's life and encouraging me as I eased into it.

Thank you to the friends who helped keep me sane over the last several years, especially Melissa Zentgraf, Sarah Nuccio, and Jen Curry.

Thank you to my parents, Lynn and Joyce Torbeck, for supporting me in every way possible, and modeling how to raise a complex kid and still laugh.

Thank you to my brother, Dave Torbeck, for showing me that a complex kid can grow up to be an amazing adult, and for giving me a sister when he married his gorgeous and brilliant wife Diane.

And infinite thank yous to Tom and the boys, for their love, support, and unending supply of hysterical source material. My life is forever changed because of the three of you. I love you.

Introduction

Wouldn't it be great if there were a handbook for raising gifted and twice-exceptional kids? Not descriptions of them, because we already know those from living with them, but something more. Perhaps coping skills for when they prove, yet again, that they are smarter than their parents. Or, how to keep your cool when advocating for their social, emotional, and educational needs. Or, what to do when their asynchrony and over-excitabilities butt heads at the worst possible moment. Yeah . . . a handbook of practical assistance with a 24-hour helpline.

This is not that handbook—and I screen all my calls. Sorry.

What you will find here is humor, compassion, frustration, astonishment, and the eerie sense that I live in your closet. I am not interested in living in your closet—unless it is a floor to ceiling wine cellar with high-speed internet and the guarantee of uninterrupted thought; for that, I'll let your call go through.

As different from the general population as our kids are, we parents experience many of the same issues as we raise them. We feel alone, accused of being "elitist" for advocating for our kids, accused of bragging when simply talking about them, and accused of pushing our kids when, in reality, they are pulling us behind them at a high rate of speed. It can be lonely. Add in the natural quirkiness and challenges of a gifted or twice-exceptional kid, and even extended family may not believe what we go through.

Too many parents find that their kids struggle with school, other kids, and life in general. My oldest son did-does. His out-of-the-boxness is why, midway through writing this book, we brought him home to be homeschooled. It's not something I ever envisioned, but was the best educational decision for him. By the time we pulled him to homeschool, he had been in three elementary schools in six years. The last school was the result of a cross-country move, and was a much more difficult transition for him than we had anticipated. While I wish traditional school could have worked out, I have never regretted the decision to homeschool.

You will not feel alone here. So, unwrap the good chocolate from the hidden stash, lock that bathroom door, and enjoy what is most definitely not a handbook on how to parent a gifted or twice-exceptional kid.

Chapter 1

Connecting the Dots

Again, you can't connect the dots looking forward; you can only connect them looking backwards. So you have to trust that the dots will somehow connect in your future. You have to trust in something—your gut, destiny, life, karma, whatever. This approach has never let me down, and it has made all the difference in my life.
~Steve Jobs, Stanford University Commencement Speech, 2005

I've been asked so many times how and when we knew our oldest son was gifted. And every time, this quote comes back to me. We didn't know. Looking back now, the signs are so very obvious, but at the time we just knew something was "off." I started teaching and caring for young kids when I was 12, so I had some 15 years of young childhood experience by the time our kid came along. And still, he knocked me for a loop. Yeah, new parenthood does that to everyone, but this was beyond that. He was (and still is) just *more*. For years, before we knew of the twice-exceptionality, that was the only word I could use to describe our son. More.

As a newborn, he didn't want to sleep, and he could hold his head up early. But it was his eyes: you could just see him looking and

1

drinking it all in. Strangers would comment on how preternaturally alert he was. He inhaled books, both read to him and paging through them on his own. On his third birthday he got one of those large floor puzzles. Straight out of the box he had it assembled inside of 15 minutes—with the image facing the floor. He was a Lego maniac from the moment he could handle a Duplo. He rarely asked, "Why?" It was always, "How's it work?" He was "incessant curiosity in Crocs."

But he also hated loud noises and despised socks (I eventually made a rule that socks were required if there was snow on the ground). Transitions were murder. Leaving to go to a Mommy & Me class was often so traumatic that I just gave up on them altogether. We suspected he had ADHD at an early age, and finally figured out when he was three that the liquid dairy he'd enjoyed since age 15 months was making him even more hyper.

Looking backward, connecting the dots. Amazing intelligence with exhausting challenges. When his brother was born, we realized that not every kid was as intensely intense as he was. And we started asking questions—of friends, of his preschool teacher, of anyone we thought might have answers. What we kept hearing was how bright he was, how much he resembled a friend's son who was highly gifted, that we should have him tested. With the Gifted Development Center in Colorado just down the road from us, we took a leap of faith and had them test our four-year-old son. How did I find the GDC? A Google search. *That's* how little I knew about giftedness in 2005.

I didn't understand then what twice-exceptional was, but I sure do now. And I learn more and more about it every day. If you had asked me if I thought our son was gifted back when he was four and I wasn't sure I was going to let him live to see five, I would have laughed maniacally and dashed off to keep Mr. Curious from an investigation that would have resulted in an ER visit. Only by looking backward and connecting the dots with what I know now am I able to see the signs of giftedness that were there long before testing confirmed it.

ঙ০ঙ৩

We may not do many things right around here, but by God, we eat dinner together. It's usually later than we would like, it's often creative leftovers, it may be a hassle, but we do it. Life is only going to get more challenging as the boys get older and involved in more activities, so it's my hope that we've set the expectation that dinners are important.

At the very least, they are amusing.

<cue: boxing bells>

Always thinking, in the east corner, this boy is a Cerebral Contender. He stands 4-feet-something tall, weighing in at slightly less than the dog. He holds an amateur Brain-to-Brain Sibling Combat record of 5 wins and many losses, with a record number of draws. He is the current, reigning, and defending Sibling Irritation Champion. Thinking from long side of the dining room table:

Geographyyyyyy Boooooooy!

Aaanndd . . . warming up his brain in the south corner, this kid is a Cognitive Champ. Standing 4-feet-not-much-more tall, weighing in at dog plus stolen meal, he holds a professional Drive Parents Batsnot Crazy record of 2,000 wins and 0 losses, with 50 percent wins by knockout. He is the current, reigning, and defending Never-Ending-Questions Champion. Thinking from short side of the table:

Maaaaaath Kiiiiiid!

Are you ready to rrrrrummmmbbbllle?!?!?!

Math Kid: "Quiz me in math! I know this stuff!"

Geography Boy: "Give me some geography questions. Hard ones this time!"

MK: "O.K., what's the capitol of New York?"

GB: "That's an easy one! Albany! Your turn . . . hm . . . what's the (looks at mom for help) square root of 100?"

MK: "Ten!"

GB: "Poop you!"

Mom: "Uh, eating here! Keep it clean."

MK: "What's the capital of Idaho?"

GB: "Too hard! What's a million times a million?"

MK: "Whaaaat? No fair! What's the latitude and longitude of the Lost City of Atlantis?"

GB: "Atlantis is a myth! What's the square root of dog?"*

The entertainment quickly shifts to stand-up comedy.

MK: "Mom! How does a garden defend itself?" <doesn't wait for a reply> "With aSPEARagus!!"

GB: "Mom! What kind of dog escapes? A Harry HOUNDini!"

MK: "MOM!"

Mom: "Seriously guys, you do realize there is another adult here you could be yelling all this at, right?"

Dad: "Uh . . ."

And can't have dinner without w(h)ine.

GB: "Can I have a treat? Awww . . . why not? I ate my dinnerrrr!"

MK: "Can I have a treat? What? Why not? I ate my dinnerrrr!!!"

And that is a typical dinner here at the House of Chaos.

*For the record, the square root of dog is woof. Just in case you needed to know.

ℬℭ

And now for a little ditty.

What do you do with a Gifted Child?

To be sung to the tune of the old sea shanty, "Drunken Sailor," preferably the Irish rock version by the Dropkick Murphys.

What do you do with a gifted child?
What do you do with a gifted child?
What do you do with a gifted child?
Early in the morning?

Way hey and up he rises
Way hey and up he rises
Way hey and up he rises
Early in the morning!

Give him some Legos and pray he's quiet
Give him some Legos and pray he's quiet
Give him some Legos and pray he's quiet
Early in the morning!

Throw him at the bookcase for some learning
Throw him at the bookcase for some learning
Throw him at the bookcase for some learning
Early in the morning!

What do you do with a gifted child?
What do you do with a gifted child?
What do you do with a gifted child?
Early in the morning?

Way hey and up he rises
Way hey and up he rises
Way hey and up he rises
Early in the morning!

Google his questions while you gulp coffee
Google his questions while you gulp coffee
Google his questions while you gulp coffee
Early in the morning!

Send him off to school and hope they teach him
Send him off to school and hope they teach him
Send him off to school and hope they teach him
Early in the morning!

What do you do with a gifted child?
What do you do with a gifted child?
What do you do with a gifted child?
Early in the morning?

ഇൻൽ

Once upon a long time ago, I could stand in a lonely practice room slogging away with my flute for hours on end, making tiny improvements that would take months to notice. I'd take a break every couple of hours or so, but the name of the game was Intense Focus, and the prize more hard work. It was awesome. I cannot imagine such a scenario today.

I am convinced I have adult-onset, child-induced ADHD. Since my oldest son was born, I have been entirely unable to concentrate on one thing for longer than a few minutes. He has trained me to have the focus of a Golden Retriever playing catch with a yo-yo. Even while putting these words on paper, my mind is trying to convince me to reboot the laundry, see why my son is whooping it up outside, check my email, get more iced tea, check the time, chew my nails, and empty the dishwasher. My brain has been trained over the last several years to shun focus, because when you focus *something happens*.

<cue ominous music>

Something like your two-year-old son escaping from a second-floor condo to search for you out by the garage and your finding him running barefoot through a busy parking lot.

Something like discovering that your five-year-old and two-year-old sons enjoyed a granola fight in the younger son's crib. With a Costco-sized box of granola.

Something like hearing your six-year-old son riding a piece of cardboard down the stairs like a sled, capping it off with a sprained ankle.

<end ominous music>

So I have the adult-onset, child-induced ADHD for good reason. I focus, something goes awry. This is why I get squat done when the boys are around: I'm waiting for something to happen. By the time they're in bed, and I can almost maybe concentrate, I'm exhausted from the daily vigil of expectation.

It's just, well, I miss my brain. We used to go for long walks through thoughts together. Double-dated with new ideas. We used to dive into activities and barely take time to come up for air. Now my brain is crashed out on the mental couch, drooling a little, while I perch anxiously, waiting to spring into action, my Mom Radar spinning wildly 24/7. We try to spend quality time together, but that must send off some sort of parental pheromone. We start to get cozy and suddenly small male creatures are bouncing around crying, "Mom? Mom! Moooommmmm!!!!" Or the Mom Radar screeches into DANGER MODE (remember: silence is the enemy) and the mood is lost.

I'm hopeful that the adult-onset, child-induced ADHD is a temporary condition. That the cure is *Children Moving Out, 2 mg*, or at the very least, *Children at Summer Camp, 2 wk*. There are no interim treatments, no sanitariums, no rest for the weary.

There was something else, but I lost my focus.

ജ‍ഗ

Sometimes I just want to shout from the rooftops:

Here is what I wish the world knew about parenting 2e kids!

Lists keep chaos at bay, so enjoy ten no-holds-barred, painfully honest, please-know-I-mean-well points. Oh, and while I know I don't speak for everyone, I plan to use the royal "we" enough to drive us all nuts.

1. Friends, teachers, acquaintances, extended family, and random people on the street, bear with me, accept this with the love I'm throwing with it. Here we go. Deep breath. *We're not making up this stuff.* We really do have gifted kids who have various issues that hold them back. Yes, it exists. You can have a highly gifted kid with processing speeds slower than molasses/Sensory Processing Disorder/ADHD/anxiety/school underachievement. Highly gifted is not the same as high achieving. Highly gifted is how a person is wired, not what a person produces. Please remember this.

2. Parenting twice-exceptional kids is more exhausting than you could possibly imagine. We are ON all the time. We never know what will ‑crop up, or when or where or how our 2e kid will react. "Constant Vigilance!" is our motto. We have to support and encourage the racing gifted mind (which is often several miles ahead of us), while at the same time nurturing the part of the kid that is struggling. Oh,

and we have to have answers for every question thrown at us: Dr. Google and I are besties.

3. These 2e kids of ours are expensive. Therapy, medications, special diets for sensitive systems, more therapy, doctor appointments, specialized evaluations, therapy again—all stuff not covered by insurance. . These are not extra-curricular activities, these are life skills they're missing and need. Classes, camps, computer programs, museum memberships, books, books, and more books. Repair and/or replacement of home items fallen victim to "scientific investigations." Clothing without tags and seams, weighted blankets, . . . you get the idea We just hope and pray our kids get full scholarships to college or invent something mind-blowing and make a fortune. And then remember us fondly.

4. Sometimes we appear over-protective, while sometimes we seem neglectful. Over-protective because our kids are so asynchronous that we're never quite sure what age we're dealing with at any given time. Neglectful because a) they need to suck it up and learn skills that challenge them without our holding their hands through it and b) see #2.

5. While we may joke that twice-exceptional means "exceptionally gifted and an exceptional pain in the neck," that doesn't mean anyone else can say that. Live the life before those words escape your lips.

6. These kids abhor change, any kind of change. Change of plans, change of location, change of anything. Surprises can chuck carefully laid plans straight into the abyss. Yet they crave novelty. This seesaw of intensity is like playing tug of war with a black hole: you don't get anywhere and eventually someone is going to get crushed.

7. Not every 2e kid has the same issues. Every single one of these kids presents differently, and they are not in parenting magazines or

books, mainstream blogs, or general societal acceptance. So when we find other parents in the same leaking boat, bailing water with a cracked Styrofoam cup, we're thrilled. We're not living the exact same lives, but they are close enough that we can relax a little bit when we all get together, knowing that we're not going to be judged by people who just don't get it.

8. Sometimes, in our ugliest and darkest days, we wonder why we had kids. We rail at the universe, wishing for a different, more normal life, feeling guilty for those painful thoughts. Deep, dark, disturbing thoughts we work to keep silent. They bubble to the surface after those interminable days of non-stop intensity, never knowing what is going to pop up when or where. Again, see #2. We stay packed for those unexpected guilt trips.

9. We will go to the ends of the earth for our 2e kids, and do so nearly every day. For the record, the ends of the earth aren't all that exciting—pretty dry and dusty and lots of beige. I've racked up quite a few emotional frequent flyer miles going there and back. I love my sons with a passion that takes my breath away. Still, I envy the "normal" family. The one that can go out for ice cream without worrying if there's something non-dairy available. The one that has the time and money and emotional energy to go on vacations without returning more depleted than before departure. The one that doesn't have to deal with all this craziness every day all day, with very few people understanding what it's like. I accept that normal is "just a setting on a washing machine," but when one of my most treasured memories is a Mother's Day when we went to the zoo, where, for just a few hours, we were a "normal" family, well—I'd like our standard setting to be a little more "normal" and a little less "heavy duty."

10. 2e parents just want some understanding and acceptance. Our kids aren't always being rude when they interrupt. Their one-track minds have likely gotten over-excited and they simply must share

what they know rightthisveryinstant. Our kids aren't always immature; their executive function abilities are struggling and sputtering like a car in need of a tune-up. And our kids aren't stupid because they're gifted and not the top of the class. They work so hard, every day, on the little things that so many others take for granted. Their giftedness masks their disabilities, their challenges hide their giftedness. These kids are amazing and they are going to change the world.

So there you have it. Ten things I want others to know about parenting twice-exceptional kids. I know other parents may have a different list, but this one is mine. This isn't a road I ever expected to travel; heck, I didn't even know this road existed! It's bumpy, full of potholes and ruts, but the view at the end of the road is stunning. These are incredible kids.

Chapter 2

One Heck of a Ride

I'm sure most parents of gifted kids have heard at one point or another, "Must be nice to have a gifted child."

Riiiiiight...

That's a classic case of comparing insides to outsides. They see a young prodigy or a precocious speaker or an early reader or a child who can talk in great detail about topics that confuse adults and think *Wow, that's amazing. Things come so easily to him. Must be nice.*

Riiiiight...

So let's play the game the other way.

Must be nice to have a child whose racing brain doesn't keep her awake into the wee hours.

Must be nice to have a child who doesn't respond to every simple request with demands to know the logic behind the request, in full detail, signed and dated in triplicate.

Must be nice to know that the school will not only provide a Fair and Appropriate Education, but that the only reason you'll ever get a phone call is because he's running a fever.

Must be nice to not have to worry about your child making and keeping friends.

Must be nice to not wonder what little thing will trigger a full-scale meltdown, courtesy of over-excitabilities and gifted intensities.

Must be nice to take your kid somewhere new and not worry about having to leave early because of over-stimulation.

Must be nice to have the option of both parents working full-time, so there's money for vacations and college accounts and retirement savings, instead of one parent feverishly working and the other feeling guilty about not contributing while trying to stay one step ahead of the kid.

Must be nice to be able to talk about your kid's accomplishments without it being seen as arrogant bragging.

Must be nice to think that homeschooling is for the conservative religious or liberal hippies, or those who think they can do better than the "experts," instead of it being the only hope for a complex kid to get an education.

Must be nice that your kid doesn't get physically sick with anxiety attacks worrying about the environment, about world hunger, about death.

Must be nice that your kid is encouraged to live up to her potential, instead of being given the subconscious message that something is wrong with her.

Must be nice to have a parent-teacher conference and walk out smiling, instead of nauseous and wondering what to do next.

Must be nice to know that your kid will more or less be O.K., instead of knowing the drop-out, drug use, and suicide rates of gifted kids.

Must be nice to look at someone raising a gifted child and think you know what it's like.

Must be nice.

Must be nice.

14

So, you have found out your kid is twice-exceptional! Congratulations, sort of. You're in for one heck of a ride, definitely. And, you have no idea what to expect, certainly.

There's no need to fear! ChaosMom is here!

Sorry. Underdog reference. No idea why that popped in there. I'll try not to do it again.

You finally have an idea of what on God's Green Earth is going on with your kid, but now what? What's the next step?

I have no earthly idea. We've known for some time now that our son was 2e, and I'm still fumbling around in the dark. That said, there are some things to keep in mind. Ooh! A list!

1. Every twice-exceptional kid is different. They are more unique than snowflakes, change more often than a supermodel, and are less predictable than airline fares. What works for one kid may not work for another, and what worked for you yesterday may not work tomorrow. Fun, yes? (No, not really.) The fun compounds when you have more than one 2e kid. Then you're just juggling fiery chainsaws and hoping for the best.

2. Asynchrony is the name of the game. This is normal. Mostly. You're not dealing with Dr. Jekyll and Mr. Hyde here, just asynchrony. And the larger the spread between the kid's intellectual/chronological/emotional ages, the more asynchronous he is. Underachieving gifted kids are especially asynchronous, often due to learning disabilities. The tough part is reacting to the age your kid is currently displaying, especially when several ages come whipping past, one after another. That is mental parenting whiplash, and the only cure is a locked room and soothing music. Straight jacket optional.

3. As you are dealing with the alphabet soup of diagnoses that come with a twice-exceptional kid, don't forget the exceptionally gifted part. It is too easy to focus solely on the challenges that so loudly

demand attention. Feed that gifted wiring, in whatever ways it begs to be fed. You know your kid; you know what lights her up. Feed that. Watch your kid come alive and not be hindered by the various challenges she has.

4. But, do not forget these are kids. They need to run and play and be ignored by their parents. (No, really. I am not their playmate, they do not need me every minute of the day, and they are perfectly capable of entertaining themselves.) They will act like bratty kids, which gets difficult because now you're wondering, "Is this an asynchronous age issue, or did my kid just mouth off to me like other kids his age? Did he just act 'normal'?!"

5. If you think your kid needs accommodations at school, ask for them. Nicely. Before school even starts, sit down with the teacher with a list of what works for your kid. Shave months off of "Learning What Makes This Kid Tick." Bake something for the teachers, be a presence in the school. The teachers have more on their plates than you'll ever know, and they'll love you for being on their side, especially as you are asking them to be on your side.

6. Get your kid a mentor. Why? Besides the fact that it is someone working with your kid on something he loves, it gets you off the hook for a little bit every week. And every kid needs an adult, other than a parent or teacher, who is interested in his life. I was that mentor for so many kids when I taught flute lessons. It's important. And people who understand your kid's arcane interests will be happy to listen to him ramble on and on, without their eyes ever once glazing over.

7. Assemble resources. Need OT[1]/VT[2]/tutoring/therapy? Ask around for referrals. Create your own little posse of professionals. They will make your life easier.

8. Finally, find your tribe. We are out there, other parents of 2e kids. We are hiding in plain sight, but if you use the gently probing key

words ("extremely bright," "intensely challenging," "more, more, more"), you will find us. We just don't talk about giftedness and its wiring and the complex challenges of raising 2e kids with random parents because they just don't get it. Unless you live it, you simply don't get it. You can find us buying wine by the box, coloring our gray hairs, and screaming when alone in the car. There's always room in the 2e Parenting Clubhouse, and you need others with you on this journey so that you don't feel so alone.

So, there you go. Welcome to the club. We're all in this together. Pull up a chair, pour some wine, and let's toast our incredible twice-exceptional kids.

---

[1] *OT: Occupational therapy. Develops, recovers, or maintains the ability of the child to perform daily living, learning, and work skills. (Please see www.giftedhomeschoolers.org/definitions.html for more information.)*

[2] *VT: Visual therapy. Develops, recovers, or maintains the ability of the child to perform visual tasks. (Please see www.giftedhomeschoolers.org/definitions.html for more information.)*

ഇരുന്

Dear Teacher:

Hi. My child is going to be in your class this year. He will be one of many kids you will teach for the next several months, but I guarantee this child of mine will be the one you remember. You will win "I Can Top That" drinking games for the rest of your career. He will have you stopping at Starbucks every morning for caffeinated reinforcements/taking up Super Ultimate Kickboxing for stress relief/planning your sabbatical before Back to School Night. I'm way ahead of you, thwarted only by the fact that parents don't get sabbaticals. Pity, really.

You and I are going to be become very close this year, and it's not an entirely good kind of closeness. Educational Frenemies.

Adversarial Allies. Compatible Opposites. We both want what's best for this kid, but, well, one of us is coming from a place of detached bureaucracy, and the other from a place of raw, unfiltered exhaustion.

Please believe me when I tell you that he is like no other student you've ever had. I can see in your eyes that you don't believe me. I can see you're thinking, "I'm an experienced teacher. I've sat through lifetimes of boring Professional Development. I know what I'm doing. I don't need this myopic helicopter mom giving me advice." So please don't take offense when I discreetly snicker with "I told you so" overtones when you confess in late October that "he is the most complex kid I have ever had in my career."

My son is the epitome of an Out of the Box Thinker. He will make you a better teacher, if you simply join him outside the box. I know that's difficult; state testing is the packing tape holding that box shut. You have too many students, not enough time, and there's just no money to do anything different. I get it, I really do. Once upon a time I was a teacher myself. But just as you know how to teach a classroom, I know how to reach this kid.

Listen to what I have to say. Take to heart what I will share with you this year. Trust that I wouldn't tell you how he learns unless I thought it would help you help him. I don't like confessing his challenges and vulnerabilities, and do so only so that we're both at the same starting gate when school begins.

So let's work together and make sure this incredible kid has a good year. It'll be tough at first—he's not a fan of change—but if you can win him over, he'll move mountains for you. The first few months you'll see a lot of those challenges and complexities, but once those have been smoothed over, the giftedness will shine through. And you will relish those glimmers as you do the sun after a bad storm.

Good luck. We're both going to need it.

Best to you,
Jen

ಬಿೀಲಕ

If I ran a Gifted and Talented Conference, it might sound something like this:

<Introduction>

<Applause>

Welcome to the 15th Annual Everything Gifted and Talented Conference! So glad you could make it back this morning for another full day of all things gifted. Before we start, a few housekeeping items.

The meeting room for the "Comfort Food and Wine Pairings after Coping with a Child's Emotional Meltdown" has been moved to the Main Ballroom, after yesterday's overcrowded session ended in fisticuffs. We would like to apologize for so badly underestimating the popularity of this session. If you are able, please contribute at the registration desk to the Friends and Colleagues Bail Bond Fund.

Again, many thanks to our sponsors for the year's new soundproof frustration rooms: Joe's Boxing and More for the headgear, gloves, and punching bags; Neal's Smash-O-Rama for the bats, eye protection, and wide variety of Hummel figurines; and Dina's Vocal Studio for the guidance in primal scream therapy.

Please remember to sign up for a massage! There are NO walk-ins! We have every available massage therapist in the metro area, and their times are filling up. Wait, what's that? Sorry, just received word that every slot is filled. Please! Sit down! No need to riot! Oh, and if you know where they are, kindly return the My Happy Place aromatherapy reed diffusers to their rightful place, no questions asked.

O.K., before I begin my presentation on "Appreciating the Absurdities of Parenting and Teaching GT Kids," let's see who is in the audience this morning.

Teachers? Raise your hands? Hmm, not that many this morning. Remember, please donate to the Friends and Colleagues Bail Bond Fund at the registration desk; we need the teachers back in their classrooms. Oh, wait—maybe they're enjoying the peace and quiet.

Administrators? Hi guys. Good to see you. And despite the concern over your dwindling numbers here, there is simply no truth to the rumor that you're being auctioned off to research labs for GT budget funds. Federal and state legislators are being auctioned off; the administrators are simply overseeing the process to ensure fair market price. Good news! The politicians who voted, again, to cut funding for gifted education went for a suh-weet price yesterday! In fact, we got such a great price for them that not only is all funding restored, but every GT program budget nationwide will be increased by 42 percent!

And, finally, parents? No, not parents who are here as teachers or administrators. Just parents who are here as parents. Hmm, more than I expected. You guys are the duct tape that holds it all together. I suspect you're here for one of three reasons. You're here because this is a passion area for you—you want and need to know all you can about giftedness so as to better parent and advocate for your children. Or you're here because you are looking for someone who has The Answer. Or you're here because you heard that there would be a child trade-in program. The trade-in program was replaced by the legislator auction this year, sorry to disappoint you.

Dealing with gifted kids can be just exhausting. Teachers? Administrators? You have no idea what anguish parents go through raising these intense kids. You think you do, but unless you're raising one yourself, you really just don't know. Parents? You have no clue what teachers and administrators put up with as educators. You think you do, but unless you're in that profession, you really just don't know. O.K, are we all on the same page now?

But I'd like to address the majority of my comments here to the parents. And—I'm already getting the "hurry it up already" sign from DeeDee down here in front with the timer. DeeDee, I'll do the best I can. This 96-slide Power Point presentation won't show itself. But if you're interested, you can find the entire thing on my website.

Back to parents.

Parents, you need to remember to take care of you. I know as well as anyone that putting yourself first appears selfish, but to heck with that. If you're falling apart, you cannot support, care for, and advocate on behalf of your complex children. Please remember that they're going to pick your nursing home, so kindly ensure that they have the ability to make solid and well-considered decisions.

You are not alone. There are so many of you out there, most of you flailing wildly. You need to band together. Gather, have coffee, and support one another. Laugh at the absurdities of your lives! Have an enormous family day where you throw all the kids together with cardboard boxes, a candle nub, a dozen rubber bands, and a pencil, and see what they create.

Get involved. Join your state's GT organization. Join the local affiliate. Create one if you need to! Start a parents' group at your school. One voice is whining; many voices is a statement.

DeeDee, quit jumping up and down, I see you. I'm wrapping up. Can any of the parents out there use your favorite OT strategy to calm her down? She's not a minor; duct tape is an option.

Thank you for the opportunity to speak with you this morning, it was truly my pleasure. Now allow me to introduce our next speaker, Mike O'Connell Ramirez Shapiro, who will present "1001 Funny Voices to Snap Your Kid out of a Freakout."

✄

As I was idly scrolling through Facebook one morning, which I tend to do as I suck down the remaining dregs of that life-giving brew, a post from *2e Newsletter* came across my feed:

QUOTE OF THE WEEK. "These children truly are exceptional. Not only are they gifted, but they are also coping with learning challenges or disabilities. It is our responsibility to give these students the extra assistance they need to become successful."
~Tom Luna, Superintendent of Public Instruction, Prologue to Students With Both Gifts and Challenges or Disabilities, published by the State of Idaho

Two things came to mind as I read this. One, if you have a twice-exceptional child and don't have a subscription to this newsletter (for more information, please go to the Resources appendix at the end of this book), hang your head in shame and toddle on over and get one. Yes, I have a subscription, and no, I don't always read it. Why not, you ask? The same reason as with all my other gifted books/magazines/newsletters: by the time I finally duct-tape the boys into bed and collapse on the sofa for a few minutes of delicious silence before the stress of the day pulls me under for the third time, I just don't have the mental stamina to read about what I just survived.

Where was I? Oh, yeah. Thought number two. This quote came from a superintendent, which not only stuns me, but delights me deeply and gives me hope that maybe someday 2e kids will be recognized as gifted *and* as working incredibly harder than other kids, in an attempt to appear merely average.

My son wasn't accepted into the district's Gifted and Talented (GT) program. Because his test scores weren't high enough, the powers-that-be decided that he would be best served in his community school and not the self-contained GT program at a separate elementary. Never mind that I have a full workup from the Gifted Development Center which states very clearly that my son would best be served in a full-time gifted classroom. Unfortunately, I unexpectedly learned this from the principal as my son was standing there, so not only did I not have the opportunity to argue effectively, but I also had the added pleasure of talking my hysterical son off the ledge once we got into the car. Oh yes, that was a joyful afternoon.

This tells me that the district's GT program is more for high-achievers, and not exactly for gifted students. Gifted students can be high-achievers, but not all high-achievers are truly gifted. I swear I'll say it until my lungs hurt, but *gifted is wiring*. Parents who desperately want gifted kids really want high-achieving kids, because if they truly had gifted kids with the (hmm, what descriptor shall I use?) *interesting* wiring, they'd be rocking under their desks, quivering like the rest of us. It ain't all sunshine and roses, folks. Some days make me want to stab a rainbow.

There is no wrong way to be gifted. It just sticks in my craw (what is a craw, exactly?) that most gifted programs aren't usually for the kids who truly need them: the ones with the asynchronous development, who struggle with basic math skills while easily grasping the properties of statistics, who can mentally design elaborate projects but can't get the ideas out on paper because they jam up on the way out. These issues—this wiring—is not easily accommodated in a traditional classroom. One of my son's beloved teachers (whom I wanted to clone and keep forever and ever) even said something to the effect *that traditional education isn't set up for this kind of kid*. He wasn't making excuses, but was upset that this was the case and that he was nearly powerless to do anything about it. Twice-exceptionality just jacks up everything by the power of ten. Even I sometimes have a hard time believing my son is gifted/2e, and I live with the kid.

To recap: It is wiring. Get a subscription to the *2e Newsletter*. There's no wrong way to be gifted—ever. And I promise I won't stab a rainbow today.

Chapter 3

Taking the Leap

How to make a difficult decision in 100 steps

1. Recognize that there is a "situation" and a decision needs to be made. This is important.

2. Fret.

3. Research online until Dr. Google is begging for respite. You have wine, you're on a mission, so Dr. Google can suck it up (not your wine, though).

4. Worry.

5. Hit the library and borrow every book that is remotely connected with <topic>. Make requests from InterLibrary Loan until the librarian asks if you are starting your own <topic> BookMobile.

6. Indulge in a mild anxiety attack.

7. Flip through the entire case of books you borrowed from the library. Attempt to read. Lose the ability to focus your mind on anything. Put the books under the pillow in an attempt to learn through dream-induced osmosis.

8. Lose sleep. Gain stiff neck. Realize you should have selected thinner tomes for the dream-induced osmosis project.

9. Email/call/talk to experts. Ask for advice.

10. Soak yourself in dread. It tastes like stale burnt coffee. And curry.

11. Drive your spouse in-freaking-sane with incessant discussion about <topic>. He will take up watching foreign indie films for peace and quiet.

12. Agonize.

13. Run to your favorite social media outlets. Kvetch about <topic>. Hold tight to any hope and humor provided by responders.

14. Brood, panic, stress the heck out, stew, torment yourself, be on tenterhooks, dwell on <topic>, get in a state, get worked up, get in a tizzy, get in a lather, get steamed up, get overwrought, get addicted to stomach acid, freak the freak out, wind yourself up, spin, and lose your everlovin' mind.

15-95. Repeat steps 1-14.

96. Hold your breath, say a prayer, light a candle, make the decision, and leap into the unknown.

97. Feel the tension release its hooks from your shoulders.

98. Follow through with the necessary steps to complete the decision-making process.

99. Notice that several weeks have gone by, you're out of groceries, the kids are wearing duct tape jeans of their own design, and the library has put a hold on your account.

100. Breathe.

ଞଠଔ

Gifted kids are not like other kids.

Oh, I'm sure that one sentence alone will upset some people. Because, you know, gifted means the child in question is smarter, prettier, more special, and more deserving. He walks on water, dispenses poop in scented plastic baggies, and has absolutely no problems with anything ever amen.

Excuse me. Sorry. Rolled my eyes so hard they shook hands with my brain. My hippocampus is looking especially robust.

So, as a refresher on what gifted is and isn't, which I need occasionally even though I live with the living/breathing/frustrating example of a twice-exceptional child, let us review.

1. Gifted kids are not like other kids. They are more intense, more curious, more everything. When we didn't know what was going on with our son, lo those many years ago, the only word I could choke out was "more." He was just *more*.

2. Gifted does not mean high-achieving. I'd like to make that sentence into t-shirts, sky-writing, tattoos, bumper stickers, jewelry, pasta shapes, and novelty doorbells that ring it out in a variety of languages when pressed. Just because a kid is in a GT program doesn't mean he is going to fit preconceived notions of what a kid in a GT program looks like or can accomplish.

3. Conversely, high-achieving does not mean gifted. I have heard of well-meaning parents with bright kids getting their kids into GT programs when the kid really shouldn't be there.

4. Gifted programs and accommodations are not for everyone. They are academic interventions to assist, challenge, and support kids with particular educational needs. Read that again: Academic

Interventions. Not "my kid is sooo special and did I tell you what she said and, by the way, the tissue from her most recent cold is going to be in an art show, titled "Crème de la Phlegm!" Oh, and the kids who need these academic interventions need them every day, all day, not just 40 minutes once a week, cancelled if something else comes up.

5. Gifted kids need more help than you think. No, really. They won't be just fine on their own. And they're not going to bring attention to that fact.

6. Twice-exceptional kids need an IEP[1] or a 504 Plan[2], despite what the school district might say. If private testing indicates significant twice-exceptionalities, written and binding accommodations and interventions are virtually a requirement.

7. Finally, don't assume anything about these kids. Gifted kids are not like other kids. Gifted kids are not like other gifted kids. Twice-exceptional kids are not like other gifted kids. And no twice-exceptional kid is like another twice-exceptional kid. These kids are amazing people, but they are not what you think. As soon as you think you know a kid, she is going to surprise you, and the only one standing and looking like a fool will be you.

There. I feel better now.

And I know that pretty much every one of these bullet points disappears with homeschooling.

I need to straighten out my eyes now. They just can't roll like they used to.

---

[1] An IEP (Individual Educational Plan) is designed for the unique educational needs of a student, intended to help that student reach educational goals more easily than without the specialized instruction. It is generally a part of special education.

[2] A 504 Plan is generally similar to an IEP, but ensures the student receives accommodations for academic success.

৪৩৫৪৩

Dear Teachers:

Well, we all tried. We tried to try and it just didn't work out, did it? I want to spout the oldie but goodie, "It's not you, it's me," but that wouldn't be entirely accurate. It was you, it was me, it was the set up of traditional school, it was accommodations taking a backseat to more evaluations, and it was the square peg that took one look at that round hole and finally declared, "No. No more."

So we're pulling our square peg from school and jumping into the adventure of homeschooling. It may come as a surprise, but I'm sure you also recognize that it's really the best course of action for him right now. See, you observe a kid in your class not paying attention and not listening; I see that same child losing his love for learning because his needs aren't being met. Not an accusation, just a statement of fact. He moves at a different pace, down a different path, to the beat of an asynchronous drummer only he can hear. I am making my peace with that; traditional school doesn't get that luxury.

I'm sure you're concerned that I'm not qualified to teach him. I could flash my teaching certificate and licensure in two states, but that really isn't necessary. See, you may be able to teach a bunch of kids, but only *I* know how to reach this one. I don't plan to teach lessons or books, I plan to teach *the child*. Again, a luxury traditional school doesn't have.

We don't know how it's going to go, or if/when he'll return to school. I have no idea what kind of curriculum we'll use, or if we'll just study what is interesting at the time. What we do know, however, is that we're done trying to make our son into someone he isn't, done trying to make him fit into a mold that really isn't necessary for life. The kid is going to change the world, but it's going to be on his terms.

So it's my turn now. I am nervous, excited, terrified, and hopeful about this new adventure. We're convinced it's the right decision for our family at this time, and are making a lot of sacrifices to make this work. This is not a decision we made lightly, not by a long shot. But there's no way homeschooling could possibly be more stressful to our son and our family than traditional school was these last few months.

We're all going to be okay.

Best to you,
Jen

₧₧

What is said: Your child is the most complex kid I've ever seen.
What is meant: I really have no freaking idea what to do.
What is heard: Whew, I'm glad I'm not you. In fact, I think I may voluntarily sterilize myself and adopt a bunch of feral cats. I'd rather be the Crazy Cat Lady, than risk having a kid this complex and intense.

What is said: We would like to administer the WISC-IV to your child again, even though these scores are only two years old.
What is meant: This is step 1.264(j)-CYA of the IEP Cha Cha that we have to perform for the state.
What is heard: Not only do we think you found a sympathetic psychologist from whom you were able to "buy" this score, but we're pretty confident your kid has gotten dumber in the last two years.

What is said: Your child refuses to participate in any class activities and will not put down a single word, even when given the words to write.

What is meant: Your kid is the most passive-aggressive ODD child I've ever known and I haven't the slightest clue how to motivate him. I am now questioning my career choice and reason for living.

What is heard: Your parenting skills are just below those of a psychotic hamster.

What is said: Public school just isn't set up for this kind of kid.

What is meant: I'm so sorry, my hands are tied. I really wish I could do more for this incredible kid, but there's only so much time, money, and effort to go around. He is amazing and it kills me that I can't do more.

What is heard: You are so screwed. You really might want to start investigating private schools or homeschooling, because he is just going to struggle more and more.

What is said: Your son has a hard time paying attention in class, following directions, and completing assignments.

What is meant: I spent more time redirecting this child in the last ten days than I did training my cat to use the toilet.

What is heard: Can this kid concentrate on anything? Does anything motivate him? Wait, he's already *on* medication for ADHD? Are you sure? Really? Have you given any thought to doubling it? It's a good thing breathing is an automatic response or you'd be the parent of a large doorstop.

What is said: He doesn't qualify for the Gifted and Talented program, but we'll supplement and differentiate in the classroom.

What is meant: Your son wouldn't be able to handle the high volume of work the program requires, because it is for high-achieving students and not necessarily for gifted kids. Twice-exceptional kids are like leprechauns: capable of causing all kinds of trouble, but we don't think they really exist.

What is heard: We'll supplement on our terms, but because he struggles with ABC and XYZ, we have to focus on improving those and not challenging his mind.

What is said: We want what is best for your son, so wish him the best of luck. Please let us know if we can provide assistance now or in the future. He's a good kid and we're going to miss him.

What is meant: Oh thank God, he's not our problem anymore! Huzzah!

What is heard: Good luck with your homeschooling adventure. You're gonna need it.

෨෪

I was not going to be a homeschooler. Well, let me back up. Back in the halcyon days of being newly married with no children, my husband and I were convinced we'd homeschool our eventual kids. We were both teachers then and felt we could do better.

Then we had children. And lo! Reality smacked us upside the head with a child who was as high-needs and intense as they come. I finally breathed three years later when he started preschool. An end to the non-stop "how's it work?" questions, the incessant motion, and the need for endless stimulation. With a newborn joining the circus, I couldn't keep up, so off to the world's greatest preschool he went.

All was well in school-land for several years—until it wasn't. Like the girl with the curl who was either very, very good or was horrid, so was school for our twice-exceptional son. Once school got to the horrid level for him, there was no way to return to very, very good. Homeschooling was always the nuclear option for us. We kept it way up high on a shelf, dusted it off occasionally, but basically tiptoed around it. We knew once we used it, there was no going back.

The three months before we pulled him to homeschool were three of the darkest months in our parenting memory. The anxiety and stress over school was incredible. I could not breathe, I could not think, I could not sleep. It was horrible. We watched our son start to wither before our eyes as his anxiety over school got worse and worse. He had always kind of liked school, had always done reasonably well, but we had just moved cross country and the change did him in. He received no gifted services, but a whole lot of interventions for the other half of twice-exceptional. No one was happy, and it was ugly.

As soon as we notified the school that he was to be homeschooled, effective immediately, the tension disappeared. The anxiety that was wracking our son was gone. I could breathe again, and was no longer having marathon sobbing sessions in the middle of the night. We could feel the whole family backing away from the brink. It was a terrifying relief. We had no idea what we were doing or what was going to happen next, but we knew we had made the right decision.

My new obsession became homeschooling research. With the little available time I had, I read books, scoured websites, harassed my poor homeschooling friends with panicked questions, and tried to reconcile what I knew about my son's learning style with what I learned about homeschooling. Per usual, little in common.

It would be so easy (for me) to purchase a single curriculum and progress through it at a steady pace, but this was The Most Complex Child on the Planet™. It soon became very clear that a more relaxed, curiosity-driven style was the way to go. The further out of his way I got, the more he wanted to learn. If I dared try to *teach* something, you could practically hear the mental gates slam shut. The happy medium was to guide and coach, but let him drive. Painful for this borderline control freak former teacher.

To date, so far, so good. For someone who had pretty forcefully decided that she was *not* going to homeschool, I sure found myself not only content with homeschooling, but happy with a more relaxed, unschooling approach. My son just keeps on teaching me, if I just get out of his way.

Chapter 4

Our Grand Homeschooling Adventure

Craves change, needs routine!
Craves change, needs routine!

Sound familiar?

I really shouldn't be surprised that our oldest is wired this way. He loves novelty, but routines and traditions are vital to him. I'm much the same way. I'm all right with change (I just abhor uncertainty), but need things in my life to be fairly predictable. Ask me how much of my life is predictable. So with the two of us in that boat, and the other two in the family similarly wired, what do my husband and I do?

Pick us all up and move us across country.

While the move was a good thing for us overall, it was far from easy. In fact, imagine "far from easy" and then tack on infinity miles and you might come close. Maybe. It was so traumatic for the four of us, in our different ways, that I wrote off that year. I just gave up on everything and focused on making it to December 31, 11:59 p.m. The child who craves predictability had an entire year that looked something like this: pack up a good portion of the house, spend four months ready to vacate the house at a moment's notice, three of those months Daddy was in another state, leave the only community you remember, move into a house that needs a lot of work, be the new kid at school, be denied entry to the new school's gifted program, be treated as learning disabled/ADHD/difficult and not gifted, be pulled to homeschool. And that's the edited version.

Things finally started to settle once we began homeschooling. Routines were established and novelty was found in the new ways of learning. Anxiety—everyone's—plummeted. Things were not perfect but better. I doubt I would have made the leap to homeschooling had we not moved, but who knows. I'll never know for sure, but I do know that leaping into the unknown world of homeschooling was the best thing for our son, right when he needed it most.

ℰᎤᏟᏕ

I am not a patient woman. I know this about myself and barely accept it. I walk fast, I talk fast, and I want to scream when my computer isn't as caffeinated as I am. If you are driving at the speed limit or below in the left lane, my eye will begin to twitch and my sons are going to learn new words (they have incredible hearing only when I drive). Despite my musical background and experience with "small improvements over time," I want things to be better *now*. This can be a problem.

I remember when our first son was a newborn. He wasn't a difficult baby, per se, but he was none too fond of sleeping. Ever. So that meant I didn't have the pleasure of blessed slumber, either. People would tell me over and over that "it gets better when they're six weeks old, it's all right!" (Those people are Lying McLiarpants.) I grabbed onto those words like a lifeline. *Things will get better when he's six weeks old! They said!* He was about a week shy of that magical date when the lack of sleep finally caught up to me and I broke down, sobbing that it was always going to be this way and what if those people are wrong, *what do I do then?*

If I had a time machine I'd go back to that hysterical woman and give myself a margarita. Yes, nursing mom and all. Because if she'd known then what she would know a decade later, it would have broken her mind.

When my son and I started our Grand Homeschooling Adventure, I gave myself until a homeschool conference two months later to have a plan and routine in place. *Things will be better when a few months have passed!* (I'm a Lying McLiarpants, too.) The conference came and went, and I was still standing there wondering what on earth I was going to do, more confused than ever. I was also warily looking around for an older me holding out a margarita. On the rocks, with salt.

There was *no way* two months was enough time to figure out how to homeschool The Most Complex Child on the Planet™. That wasn't even enough time to deschool him. The general consensus is a month of deschooling for every year in traditional education, and two months wasn't even close. Add on the fact that he resists being taught, had forgotten how much he loved learning, has stubbornness down to an art, and that I was an impatient mess trying to figure out what to do, and you had the perfect storm for a Homeschool Freakout.

Homeschool Freakout: To lose one's mind attempting to create the perfect homeschooling situation for The Most Complex Child on the Planet™. Brought on by multiple curriculum changes, hours of internet research, worry that the child will be behind if traditional school suddenly becomes unavoidable, panic that the child will end up dumb as a bag of rocks, and the realization of *Oh My God, I'm in charge of my child's education.* Symptoms include, but are not limited to: shallow breathing, chest pains, insomnia, teeth grinding, nausea, paralysis by analysis, overdue library fines, and skull fractures from banging one's head against the wall. See also: *every beginning homeschooler ever.* Treatment depends on the individual sufferer but may include: massage, wine, chocolate, ladies' night out, deep breaths, turning off the computer, frou-frou coffee drinks, reading fiction for a change, sending the offspring to the grandparents for the weekend, journaling, meditation and prayer, talking to experienced homeschool parents, exercise, patience, and wine. Successful recovery from a Homeschool Freakout depends on several factors, most importantly the ability to just get a dang grip already and relax. Do I do this? Heh. No. I am still in the treatment stage; I anticipate recovery after my sons move out.

Patience may be a virtue, but it's not mine. After a school situation that left us frustrated and sad, I wanted to see instant improvement, the return of the curious learner of years past. I know my son will eventually get to the point of enjoying learning again, just as he did eventually learn to sleep through the night. It'll just be on his timetable, not anyone else's. In the meantime, I'll continue Homeschool Freakout treatments and wait for our timetables to merge. I know they will; after all, I'm sleeping again. I just have to be . . . sigh . . . patient.

෮෮෮

I homeschool for a long list of reasons, and despite our challenges with school, nothing on that list has to do with a classroom teacher.

I stand with teachers.

As of this writing, Chicago teachers are considering a strike. They are in contract negotiations with the district, which are not going well. I heard a radio ad that got my blood boiling. It was a "conversation" between two moms, *so* concerned that the teachers might strike. They decided that parents needed to talk to teachers and convince them not to strike, because you know, *won't someone think of the children?*

Really?

Most teachers think of the children every day. They put up with more from ignorant legislators, the general public, and parents ~~like me~~ than you know. And in return for their efforts, teachers are not treated as professionals and are paid less per hour than the going babysitter rate. Teachers are the front-line scapegoats for a very broken system.

I stand with students.

Our students are paying the price for our inability to fix the education system in this country. There's a lot of lip-service to fixing the problems, but very little is actually getting accomplished. The current factory model (throw 'em in, churn 'em out) no longer works. It was designed decades ago, when life was *much* different from today. Society has evolved, our education system has not. What we're seeing today is the result of our unwillingness to change to meet today's lifestyle. It's not a case of throwing more money at it, or more accountability, but complete and total change. I don't know what a new system would look like, but it's sure not what we have today. It obviously doesn't work.

I stand with parents.

Parents are trying to pick up the slack, filling in the holes of their kids' educations because the education system is struggling. I straddle both the homeschooling and the public schooling worlds, so I see this so clearly. Art and music and physical education continue to be cut, to allow for more ~~test prep~~ instructional time. The amount of homework an elementary school student brings home at night is well more than I had at that age. And parents are caught in the middle. So many work long hours to provide (among other things) the music and art and sports experiences their children are missing at school, then have the pleasure of supervising homework with a child who just did eight hours of "sit in your seat, don't talk, don't fidget" school. My friends with traditionally educated kids are frustrated. When do the kids get to play and be kids? When are families supposed to have family time? And how is a kid supposed to do all this and still be in bed by a decent hour? The demands placed on an elementary school student are just too much, and are creating more and more stress on them and their families.

I believe the education system in this country is deeply flawed and should be completely overhauled. The current set up suits no one. Teaching to the test is insane. The only learning going on is how to pass the test, not how to think or to question or to create. When our oldest son was in public school, he would come home in late spring so excited to have *learned* something, because state testing was over for the year. All the months leading up to that point either were things he already knew or had a lot of test prep. So wrong. In a generation we, as a society, are going to reap what we sow, and it ain't gonna be pretty.

I am not an education expert, not by a long shot. I am a licensed teacher, I am a parent, and I am a home educator. But I will shout to the skies that our current education program is irretrievably broken. Parents are fed up and are voting with their feet as best they can. The rise of homeschooling and parent-driven charter schools are indicative of that. So while I homeschool one son, and it's within the realm of possibility that the other *might* be homeschooled at some point too . . .

I stand with teachers.

I stand with students.

I stand with parents.

Just not the current education system.

ᛒᛃᚷᚲᛒ

Attention New Homeschoolers!
How to Lose your Everlovin' Mind in Five Easy* Steps.

1. Don't have a plan. Wing it, every day. Skip the record keeping, the portfolios, the organization. Get up every morning, throw a

book/video/website at the kid(s), and hope that learning occurs through osmosis.

2. Be inflexible. If an opportunity arises for an educational experience, whether through a conversation or current events or (gasp!) curiosity, ignore it. If it is not in the lesson plan, it can wait until it *does* appear on the lesson plan. That the histrionics of the student(s) are interfering with learning is secondary.

Note: Yes, steps one and two are incompatible. This does not mean they cannot both occur.

3. Deny yourself. Ignore the fact that you are an adult and have your own interests, hobbies, and preferences. Skip ~~wine~~ book club, forget about the chess team, and don't even think about auditioning for a community band. All your time and energy and finances must be devoted to your student(s) and his/her/their education.

4. Stay home. It is called *home*schooling for a reason. You must only school at home. Do not leave the house for a co-op or an educational field trip. The library is for after-school hours, as are the rec center and conversations with other homeschoolers.

5. Shun all advice. You know your student(s) best, so there is no need to take advice from anyone else. No one could possibly help you, as your situation is entirely unique and thus advice would be entirely unhelpful.

There you go, folks! The sure-fire way to lose your everlovin' mind as a new homeschooler, guaranteed to produce tears, extreme doubt, and the words "What on EARTH was I thinking?!" to escape your lips.

*"Easy" and "homeschool" should never be in the same sentence, even in a tongue-in-cheek essay. My apologies.

ଈୠ୭୧

A lot of things go through your mind as you see your ten-year-old son ride an oversized office chair down the driveway towards the street.

There is the "Oh please, dearest Universe, let all crazy/distracted/teenaged drivers be anywhere but here" prayer.

There is the "Sometimes I really wish shock collars for kids were legal in this state" plea.

There is the furtive glance at the watch wondering if it was "five o'clock somewhere." Anywhere.

And there is, overriding everything else, the thought of What The _____. <Insert your favorite expletive here. I know you have one. And if you're a better parent than I, your kids didn't learn it from you.>

Just another afternoon in the House of Chaos.

Where else could you find, in one day, the aforementioned office chair joyride, an intense discussion on the merits of Brussels sprouts, rousing role play on selling Cub Scout popcorn, epic homework battles (Genghis Khan looks on from the afterlife in awe), a hot-water-heater-draining shower that ends with an advanced discussion on whirlpools (northern versus southern), and the mom collapsing from complete mental and emotional exhaustion?

And that's just Monday.

Kids are exhausting. Gifted kids are exhausting plus emotionally draining. Twice-exceptional kids are exhausting with a double side of emotionally draining, all deep-fried in guilt and smothered in a tart regret sauce. Tasty, tasty parenting.

Hooboy, the universe smacked me upside the head with my sons. I had no idea it was going to be this hard. I mean, of course it was going to be hard because it's parenting, but this hard? Not a clue. I have, on occasion, wondered just what I was thinking becoming a parent, and that perhaps raising llamas might have been a better idea. At least llamas stay out in the yard so you can retreat for a little peace and quiet. They're just not as cute on Santa's lap for the annual picture.

This life is not what I expected. I accept it (mostly—I do have my railing at the universe moments, shaking fist and all), and while I love my sons to the end of time and back, I do not love being a parent every moment of every day. It's more of a 60/40 split. On really good days, 75/25. Anyone who boasts a 100/0 split is a pathological liar or needs to share their mood-altering cocktail recipe. I thought by now I'd be enjoying it a little more and redirecting them a little less. The intensities, the insatiable curiosity, the stubbornness, the sensitivities, the asynchrony, the sensory issues, the over-excitabilities, the questioning of every single little thing, the constant demands on every cell of my being . . . they all make for some rough days, and that doesn't even take into consideration the challenge of advocating for them outside the house. There is nothing resembling cruise control when parenting a gifted kid; they are *damn the torpedoes, full speed ahead,* and you have to be on alert to make sure they don't ram into something for which they're not mentally or emotionally prepared. I refuse to blow sunshine and claim that everything is hunky-dory when in reality things tend to be more challenging than the norm. Pessimist? Realist. The glass may be half-full, it may be half-empty, but I'm certain we can both agree that it needs more <insert beverage of choice here>.

Years into this parenting gig and I'm really no closer to getting the hang of it. I know other parents of gifted and twice-exceptional kids have emerged on the other side of intense parenting nearly unscathed, and I pray that I will be one of those someday.

In the meantime, I suspect my stress about it all would be greatly reduced if I hopped on that wild office chair ride with my son, laughing all the way to the curb. That would make for a 90/10 day.

In case you were wondering, I do have a younger son. He puts up with so much. He's the calmer, quieter, more laid-back, less-squeaky wheel younger brother. That's not to say that he's always calm, quiet, and laid-back; he sure has his moments, but nothing to the intensity level of his brother. He hears his older brother meltdown when the over-excitabilities are too much, he sees his parents stressed about it more often than not, he has coping skills of someone much older.

I can relate.

My younger brother would easily be diagnosed as twice-exceptional today. For years I've laughed (sardonically) that I'm raising my brother, that the parental curse "I hope you have a child *just like you*" got mixed up in the ether. That my beautiful nephew is a laid-back happy kid just proves my point. My brother can never say his son doesn't sleep, that he has tantrums, that he's fussy. *I win, game-set-match.* My brother struggled in school, with labels like LD and ADHD and ABC and XYZ. This, despite the fact he got a higher ACT score than his older sister, who was in mainly gifted and honors classes throughout her school career. I love my brother so much, but I was so happy to leave for college. The battles, *the homework battles*, about did me in. That my eldest son and I have had homework battles to rival those is not lost on me. My own parents say that I have it harder with my first born than they ever did with my brother. Small comfort.

My parents worked their butts off to make sure I wasn't forgotten as they struggled with him. I had my own issues, but I was "easy." *Really, Jen?* Yes, really. I was grounded a grand total of once in my life. There was never a Do-or-Die meeting with the school over my performance, and I basically did what was expected of me. They came to my softball games, my concerts, my everything. Always there for me, they never let me feel that my brother's issues were so big that they couldn't.

I wish I could say that about me.

My youngest is the only person in this house who is not an introverted Type-A firstborn with all the interesting baggage that comes with that. Poor kid. He's learning some valuable life skills dealing with the three of us, that's for sure. But he's not without his challenges as well. He started speech therapy at 20 months old and got an IEP at age three. In second grade the school threw him into interventions for writing (don't get me started on how intently schools push writing at such young ages), and he started to test some "school is too haaaard" boundaries.

But even with all that, he's just . . . easier. I cut my teeth on his older brother, so nothing he does really fazes me. It just kills me that I'm not able to pull it together often enough to give him more individual attention. I try, but I feel like I'm failing, even more so now that he's still in public school while I homeschool his older brother. And I feel like I'm doubly failing as I see him start to learn some of the attention issues with which his brother struggles. I say "learn" because he doesn't have ADHD but is simply imitating his brother.

I am grateful my sons are such good friends. And I'm relieved that we don't have two off-the-charts high-intensity twice-exceptional boys. But I also wish there were two of me or more hours in a day, because I'm afraid one of my sons is getting the short end of the stick, and that both saddens and angers me. I was so fortunate to have parents who were able to support me and make me feel special, even though they also had a high-intensity kid. I only wish I felt I were doing the same for my son.

⁊⌒

I somehow became a gardener in the last decade. Sure didn't see that coming, especially since I have a hard time keeping houseplants from dying slow, dehydrated deaths. But outdoor gardening is different for some reason, maybe because I can eat the fruits of my labor. And it occurred to me that gardening is a lot like parenting a gifted child.

If you look at all that needs to be done when you're just starting out, you're going to freak out and give up. Just keep your head down, focus on what is right in front of you, and improve one little thing. Eventually you'll lift your head and be stunned at your progress.

It is hard work and you are going to get dirty. The blood, sweat, and tears involved will surprise you, but that is normal. You will also hurt, swear, and wonder just *why* you thought this was something you wanted to do. This is also normal.

You will have to deal with a lot of, ahem, manure. While it does a fine job of making things grow, it still stinks to high heaven and may keep others away. However, those living similar lives will know that it's just part of the design and will stay by your side. They may also help you shovel it. Hang on to these people: they are your greatest asset.

There will be dry spells when you'll wonder if there is any progress being made. Long, scary dry spells. Know that even during dry spells there is growth; it's just so small as to be indistinguishable.

You will spend an inordinate amount of time weeding. Weeds are simply things that thrive exactly where they don't belong. You will weed out the chokers, the ugly, the disrupters, and the harmful. And then you will do it again and again and again.

No matter how hard you toil, there is always the possibility that something will blow in and ruin the progress that has been made. Scaffolding helps things grow, by supporting in the weak times and providing strength when needed. Don't be ashamed of needing support; some plants can only grow and thrive with something on which to climb.

Sometimes you need other gardeners to help make things grow. You simply can't know everything, it's just not possible. So you'll call experts for opinions, gather with others like you for support and commiseration, and create your own tribe of like-minded gardeners.

Non-gardeners will come to you and say you're not doing it right—that you should do this or that or the other thing for more success. You don't need to listen to them; you know the soil, the growing conditions, the way the light falls better than anyone. You have your hands deep into this garden daily and know it in ways others just can't see. You're in charge, no one else.

Sadly, you won't want to talk about the magnificent things growing, because others will think you are bragging to make them feel bad about their gardens. You're not! You're just proud and happy and relieved to see them growing so well, because they're special breeds of plants that often don't thrive. In fact, it's often mistakenly believed that these plants can thrive without any assistance at all! When given all they need to grow—in the amounts they need, how often they need it—these plants reach unimaginable heights with such beautiful blooms.

Sometimes others can't see the beauty for the weeds. So they focus on the weeds to the exclusion of everything else, damaging the blooms in the process. They won't acknowledge the blooms, because how could anything so magnificent grow with such weeds around? The weeds will be pulled and sprayed, while blooms will be ignored and not given the nutrients they need. Protect your garden. Certainly the weeds must be removed, or at the very least reduced, but not at the expense of the glorious blooms.

Finally, at the end of the day, sit back and appreciate what is right in front of you. By respecting the garden and working with it, rather than against it, you have taken a confusing mixed-bag of nature and cultivated a thing of beauty. Put your feet up and toast your garden's success.

❧❦❧

Ten Reasons Not to Strangle Your Gifted Child*

1. He's nothing if not entertaining.

2. You love seeing the stunned looks from people who are not accustomed to her verbal precocity.

3. He will grow up to change the world. Because he will grow up to change the world, there is a possibility of fame and fortune. Courtesy of the fame and fortune, he will be able to care for you in your old age, which will come about a lot faster because of his childhood. Being well cared for means you will get the good nursing home, preferably one that is located on a cruise ship sailing the globe, with sommeliers and massage therapists on call. If you're really lucky, that particular cruise ship will specialize in the parents of gifted kids. Commiseration abounds!

4. Her photographic memory means you won't have to remember pesky details, because she'll supply them. Often. With great glee.

5. His intense concern about the condition of the world and desire to improve upon it gives you hope that the world as we know it is just a little less likely to descend into chaos. Zombie apocalypse perhaps, but not run of the mill chaos.

6. If you're lucky, you'll never have to do your own tech support ever again. Be warned, this comes with a downside; it's humiliating to lose a tech argument when you used to win them against your own parents.

7. It is 31 flavors of awesome to have a geek conversation with your child. Bonus points for a Star Trek marathon while discussing the finer points of Douglas Adams during a game of chess. 42.

8. Who needs the Fountain of Youth? You will stay mentally sharp trying to stay ahead of her arguments, verbal sparring, and convoluted trains of thought.

9. You'll get to feed your own thirst for knowledge under the guise of expanding his horizons. You'll also experience all sorts of new things you never would have otherwise, due to his never ending quest for learning.

10. Someday there might be grandchildren. And then you can sit back and laugh your empty-nesting head off as you discuss wine with the sommelier before your daily massage. Karma. It's what's for dinner.

Other than: It's Illegal, Morally Wrong, and Generally Frowned Upon.

ಐ)(ೞ

MOM!? How many nanoseconds are in a century?

My reply is a slow and twisted quirking of the head as my eyebrows both rise and furrow, creating new trenches in my forehead that are surpassed only by the grey in my hair. One hand reaches for the cup of coffee, the other for my iPhone and Siri, the On-Call Personal Researcher for parents of gifted kids.

MOM!? What's the tallest mountain in the universe?

I don't mind the questions, per se, but I do mind not knowing the answers right off the bat. I love learning! I read non-fiction for fun! Why must these questions twist my brain into a Möbius strip?

MOM!? What's the biggest city in the world?

The questions are especially fun when there are multiple answers. Dear child, do you want biggest city by population, area, or a combination of the two? And why are you asking me this before I've finished my first cup of coffee?

MOM!? What's Schrödinger's Cat?

It's a physics thought experiment that has resulted in geeky cultural references and zombie kittens; they are neither dead nor alive, and they are both dead and alive. Mind Blown.

MOM!? Does Santa live at the geographic North Pole or the magnetic North Pole?

Oh, buddy. Be glad I've had enough coffee that my Santa Filter is fully attached, or we'd be having a *much* longer and intense discussion this bright and sunny morn. You'd be learning all sorts of things about the Easter Bunny and Tooth Fairy, and with your penchant for sharing whatever floats through your mind, I'd be The Most Hated Mom on the Block.

MOM!? Guess what I just learned! Do you know what quantum foam is?

Are you kidding me? Quantum foam? Please tell me it's what's floating on the top of the newest and largest Starbucks size, impossibly full of both caffeine and alcohol, available for the parents of children with mind-bending questions.

MOM!? Do black holes ever close? Or is our universe on the other side of another dimension's black hole?

My husband and I have several advanced degrees between us. Unfortunately, they are in music. That we have children who are obsessed with cosmology and detailed geography is a cosmic joke in which we are the punch line.

MOM!? Did you know that . . . MOM!? Guess what? MOM!? MOM!?

The questions melt my brain, but in the best way possible. These are the questions I can eventually answer thanks to Dr. Google, not the unanswerable ones that circle around each other as they keep me awake in the dead of night. What I find amazing and delightful is how these questions from our oldest son have increased as we've continued homeschooling. It reminds me of when he was a precocious preschooler, full of incessant questions, but now I'm better equipped to handle it and he's able to research on his own. Then again . . .

MOM!? What are breast implants?

Sigh, I'm being punked, aren't I? Seriously, where is the camera?

ℬℭ

Albert Einstein. Michael Phelps. Steve Jobs. Mark Zuckerberg. To heck with them, *what did their parents do?*

I've gotten to the point that when I hear or see amazing things done by amazing people, I clap and admire, and then direct my attention to their parents. Specifically their moms. Because there's no way on earth that was an easy kid to raise.

How on earth do we keep doing this? How are we managing to keep on keeping on? I've lost count of the number of times I've thought to myself, "I can't go on . . . I must go on." (Hat tip to Samuel Beckett.) Where is this inner strength coming from? Was there some sort of secret stamina transfusion done during childbirth? Because by rights, I should have collapsed long ago. And I know I'm not the only one. So many other moms of high-intensity or special needs kids out there are doing this, too. I don't mean to leave dads out, but let's be honest, the moms get a lot more grief and put up with a lot more junk than the dads do.

Be strong. One foot in front of the other. Stiff upper lip, tally ho, and all that nonsense (based on a quote from my mom). We keep going because we have to. There is no alternative. Who would take over if we were to falter? Or, the fantasy that must never be spoken, *to leave*? I often wonder what would happen if I just stopped caring. If I just went through the motions, instead of trying to keep all the plates spinning just so. Would all hell break loose, or would I find that I've been making myself sick with worry for no reason?

I have so many days—too many to count—when I think, "I just can't do this anymore." When I want to somehow end the chaotic life that has descended upon us for something, anything, else. But there is no *something else*. This is what we have, what we have been "blessed" with. Sorry, I can't call it a blessing with a straight face, no matter how hard I try. I strive to be grateful, but it's hard to be grateful for something you'd really love to change or exchange. And yes, I do know how selfish that sounds. Anyone who lives this life knows this feeling; anyone who *doesn't* . . . well, live this life for awhile and then let's meet up. Chances are, you'll understand my many wine references.

Someday, sooner than seems possible, our incredible kids will leave us. They will go on to live their lives without parents guiding them, ensuring their safety, teaching them that they'll survive just fine, *that they can be strong, one foot in front of the other.* I have to believe that the parents who have gone before us, those parents whose children went on to accomplish great things, went through the hell of raising intensely gifted kids by going on when they thought they just couldn't possibly handle another day. That with time, patience, and the support of great friends, they managed to love and teach and support their kids for eighteen years, without losing their minds or running like hell for the hills.

I have to believe that that's what their parents did. Because while my mom's advice rocks, it's hard to keep a stiff upper lip when you're sharing a bottle of red wine with a good friend.

Chapter 5

Living My Walter Mitty Fantasy

My all-time favorite Disney movie is Pixar's *The Incredibles.* If we're surfing through channels and it's on, don't even think of clicking away. We stay on the movie. It wasn't one of Pixar's greatest hits, but it brings me to tears nearly every time I watch it, for one simple reason:

They are a gifted family.

The entire Parr family is odd, different, complex. They have to hide their greatest abilities, for the supposed benefit of society. They all have a hard time out in the real world, because hiding their abilities is not something they can do easily. But at home, where they are safe and accepted for who they truly are, they can relax and be themselves. Sound familiar?

Mr. Incredible and Elastigirl, two very successful superheroes, marry and have kids. The apples don't fall far from the tree, so their children have their own gifts as well. Everyone in the family has his own challenge—his own over-excitability—that is both a gift and a curse. Dash has the best case of psychomotor over-excitability I've ever seen outside my own house; in the real world he'd be on a heavy dose of ADHD meds. Violet falls into both the emotional and intellectual spheres of OEs, with a dollop of teenage-angst mixed in there for giggles. And Jack-Jack . . . well, no one knows what powers he has until

53

the very end, when he demonstrates why you should never underestimate the easygoing.

My favorite scene is the one on the island where the family is surrounded by bad guys and they circle together to fight back, each relying on the others' strengths to protect their own weaknesses. This, to me, is what a gifted family does on a daily basis. They stick together, using their strengths to protect each other from the Big Bad World. Everyone's gifts are needed to survive.

What finally struck me was that the family succeeds because of their gifts and over-excitabilities, not despite them. The world wants them to hide their strengths, because society as a whole is afraid and jealous of such gifts. Not everyone has this wiring; it's misunderstood, and thus must be shunned. Only when the value of those gifts are proven are the Supers allowed to be their true selves. Well, in masked form so as to protect their secret identities, but you get the idea.

Imagine if our gifted families were lauded for their quirky and misunderstood overexcitabilities and gifts. Our kids not told that needing to move around was wrong or that deep sensitivity was a character flaw, but that these very characteristics were vital to the advancement of society. That these gifts were supported and encouraged, instead of being subliminally urged to tuck them away.

Wouldn't that be Super?

ഇരു

Before having my sons, I had it all planned out. They would be sweet, intelligent children, a joy to be around. Fluffy bunnies would hop by, birds would land on my finger to whistle duets with me, and I'd own a rainbow-farting unicorn. Well, we have bunnies, but they're of the dust variety and procreate under the couch. Birds have dive-bombed my head, worried that I was going after their nest of eggs. And I'm still waiting for my unicorn.

My boys are sweet, they are ~~almost~~ always a joy to be around, and I have had a crash course in giftedness. Before they came roaring into our lives, I believed, like most of society, that giftedness was just "super smart." The "precocious child going to med school" type of smart. But it's not. Giftedness is wiring. It's a person's inborn way of observing, interpreting, and responding to the world. It is as much a part of a person as his eye color, and neither can be changed. With that wiring comes asynchronous development, twice-exceptionality, and emotional intensities that can change on a dime.

That wiring is oh-so-fun to parent. No, not really.

Somehow I've become an accidental expert in raising gifted boys and in supporting the parents of gifted children. Too often our needs are overlooked, with "you have nothing to worry about, your children are gifted" being the typical response. These kids are not in parenting books or classes, and parents have nowhere to turn. What is normal in the gifted population is considered abnormal in the general population, and parents have little support.

I never expected to go down this gifted road, but my boys are dragging me behind them and I'm just trying to shout out directions as they disappear out of sight. The road is twisty and oftentimes full of potholes, but thankfully it appears to go through a vineyard, so I have plenty of wine to get me through this journey. It's not a bad route, just a tiring and long one with a couple of very intense drivers.

But I still want my unicorn.

ᏰᏣ᏶

I love homeschooling my son. Pulling him from school was the best thing for him, and in general it's been a good move. I don't miss the fights over homework, the breathtaking anxiety about his psyche, or the conferences with teachers about everything he was doing wrong and nothing about what he was doing right.

I hate homeschooling my son. Oh My God, it's driving me insane. I don't know if it's because he is so turned off of learning because of the time he spent in school, or if he just dislikes being taught as opposed to self-discovery, but I can't take it anymore! He is so bright and when it's something that fascinates him he'll jump in with both feet. But, oh boy, try to teach him something so he doesn't end up *living in a van down by the river!*, and we're back to the epic homework battles of ye olde school days.

I love homeschooling my son. Seeing him learn something new and then run with it to make new connections or to create from that knowledge is heartening and a relief. He is going to be fine as an adult, if we can just get him to that point.

I hate homeschooling my son. It's all on me. The good, the bad, and the oh-so-ugly. If he does well, he gets the credit; if he does poorly, I get the blame. I cannot complain about how difficult it is, or how often I want to throw in the towel and dropkick him into the nearest educational ~~factory~~ facility, because it was a decision we made and, well, you've made your bed, you'll have to lie in it.

I love homeschooling my son. We have the freedom to learn from the world around us, at his sometimes glacial pace. We have the opportunity to go on field trips with other homeschoolers, to places schools either cannot go or are not interested in going. We have the time to learn, without having to worry about state testing or never-ending fundraising or more homework after eight hours of schoolwork.

I hate homeschooling my son. I don't know what I'm doing. I'm screwing this up. Watch this video and tell me everything you learned on this notebook page in your own words. What are you doing? You're still watching videos? I don't care if it's a fascinating series on the beginnings of the universe, you've been there for hours! Let's do some math. What are you doing? You know how to do this! Good grief, you just gave me all the answers, show me how you did them so that when they get harder you'll know how to figure them out! No, you cannot watch another video. What are you doing? Yes, it's an awesome Lego candy dispenser you designed and, wow, it really does work, but you've been doing that for hours. You're not helping me here. *You can work here at home, you can work back at school, but by God you are going to work!*

Sigh. I've never had a love/hate relationship like this before. I know this was the best option for him, but there are those days . . .

શ્ Oભ

Way back in the day, when I was studying to be a professional flutist, I was on the mailing list for The President's Own Marine Corps Band. How long ago was this, you ask? It was a paper newsletter, brought to me by the United States Postal Service; not a flashy HTML e-newsletter, zipping to me through a bunch of random servers.

In it there were articles about the band, upcoming concert tours, maybe some program notes for a new piece of music. But there was always an interview with one of the band's musicians. I loved reading those, because they gave me insight into what kind of mental and intestinal fortitude it would take to actually win an audition for the President's Own. The questions rarely varied: name, instrument, hometown, college, favorite piece of music. But my favorite question was always "What is your Walter Mitty fantasy?"

Now, I love the Thurber story "The Secret Life of Walter Mitty," about an everyday man with a fanstastical imagination. It feeds into the imaginative side of me that tends to get smothered by daily life. So reading the musicians' answers to their Walter Mitty fantasy amused me. Inevitably it was something along the lines of living on a deserted island or engineering a high-speed train or having a second career as a torch singer in New York City.

Not *once* was the answer, "I'm living it." That sure would have been my answer. Your career is to play in the best wind ensemble on

57

the planet, and this isn't your secret fantasy? You didn't daydream about this while mentally hiding from day to day life? Really?

Nowadays my daydreams lean more towards a kid who responds to a simple request by, you know, *carrying out* the simple request. I can burn a whole afternoon filling in the details of that daydream, down to the decadent dessert at the celebratory dinner my husband and I would enjoy at the end of that mythical day.

But I can encourage my sons to dream those big, imaginative dreams. The ones that are so audacious as to be unthinkable. The ones that feed the soul and propel the goals. Too often today, our kids are subjected to tests and drills and You Must Learn This Because You Must Know This, and not allowed the time to dream wild dreams.

Besides, it's awfully hard to live your Walter Mitty fantasy if you've never had the opportunity to create one.

એ∞છ

"If you decide to confide in others, you'll discover you're not alone."

I first saw this line some time ago in a magazine. No attribution, just a random quote splashed in the margin. When I read it, it was as though the angels sang and the heavens opened and I got smacked with a whole lot of "duh." I had been struggling with my blog, trying to balance privacy with reaching out to others in the same boat. I didn't want to share too much and make my sons need even more therapy in the future, but I also wanted others living this life to know they weren't alone. And selfishly, I wanted to know that I wasn't alone. Delicate balance.

Although I feel like an accidental expert, I am not a real expert on giftedness or twice-exceptionality, not by a long shot. I'm barely an expert on me, and I've been around myself for <coughcough> years. My house is a living laboratory, and I'm the head researcher. I observe, test ideas, suffer through the results, and post the findings for the head researchers of other homes to read—and laugh and cry and shake their heads and give thanks that someone gets it. Oh, I get it all right. I've either lived through it or know someone who has.

Here in this House of Chaos, we've run the gamut from extreme flashes of giftedness to glaring disabilities, from wonderful school situations to those that just make your brain hurt from the lack of understanding, from things going very, very well to things going very, very badly. It can be so very lonely, made even worse when you feel you're the only one who has ever had to walk down this confusing road.

So I say, let's confide in one another. Use the code words parents of gifted kids have to use to find those who get it—words like "extremely bright" and "intensely challenging" and "my house has been overrun with Lego inventions in various stages of completion and with bad geek puns." There are a whole lot of us out there, raising these amazing kids, and we need each other, now more than ever. We're not alone on this confusing road, and if we look around, we'll see the ones who made it through and the ones just starting out. With support from each other, and a whole lotta wine, we'll make it through raising these kids with sanity to spare.

Appendix A
What is "Gifted"?

So if you're new to this party, you're probably wondering "just what is 'gifted,' exactly?"

Good question. And one that has more answers than the number of licks to get to the center of a Tootsie Roll Pop. The difference being that you can't just chomp down to get to the gooey center of *this* question.

As of this writing, the gifted community is wrestling with the definition of giftedness. Some believe it is what a person accomplishes in an educational setting, others believe it is an integral part of who a person is throughout that person's life. I believe that gifted is wiring. It's how a person observes, interprets, and responds to the world around him. Linda Silverman, of the Gifted Development Center in Denver, says it much more eloquently than I ever could:

> *Giftedness is not what you do or how hard you work. It is who you are. You think differently. You experience life intensely. You care about injustice. You seek meaning. You appreciate and strive for the exquisite. You are painfully sensitive. You are extremely complex. You cherish integrity. Your truth-telling has gotten you in trouble. Should 98% of the population find you odd, seek the company of those who love you just the*

way you are. You are not broken. You do not need to be fixed. You are utterly fascinating. Trust yourself!
~Dr. Linda Kreger Silverman (January 2012 SENGVine newsletter)

I do not believe that gifted is what a person achieves or accomplishes. If that were truly the case, I'd have a hard time explaining my own experience. At one point, I was a talented flutist. I worked my butt off, earned advanced degrees, and was going to create a successful career as a flutist. I achieved a lot, so by the gifted-is-achievement definition, I was gifted in music. But then things changed. I had kids, my priorities shifted, I developed some oh-so-fun repetitive stress injuries, and I let my flute playing fall by the wayside. Does this mean I am no longer gifted in music, because I am no longer achieving? Something to ponder.

So what is twice-exceptionality? Generally, it's gifted plus something that may interfere with the recognition of the giftedness. It can be a learning disability, ADHD, slow processing speeds, Asperger's Syndrome. . . you get the idea. It is rarely recognized and hard to understand, simply because the giftedness oftentimes masks the disability and the disability can hide the giftedness. A person is seen as average, or in need of countless interventions for the disabilities, or as someone with great potential *if only she applied herself!* Frustration is a huge component of 2e, but maybe that's only in my house.

Over-excitabilities come along for the ride in a conversation about giftedness. Polish psychologist Kazimierz Dabrowski identified five areas in which a person could react more strongly to stimuli than the norm. Those five areas are psychomotor, sensual, imaginational, intellectual, and emotional. Most gifted people present in two or three of those areas; we have the (ahem) great fortune to be raising a 2e son who presents strongly in all five. I know you're jealous.

Finally, asynchrony. For me, the hardest thing about parenting a twice-exceptional child is the asynchrony. I never know exactly which age I am dealing with at any given moment. Imagine being a young child, feeling intense despair over the state of the world, and not understanding why other kids your age (and even some adults!) don't feel the same. Or having the reading comprehension of a much older child, but lacking the maturity to deal with the topics at that level. Or knowing everything there is to know about, say, architecture, but the knowledge logjams as you try to write about it, because your writing skills lag far behind your racing intellect. In the span of a few minutes, I could have a child who looks his age, discusses cosmology and theoretical physics in great detail, whips out a few bars of his current favorite rock song, feels great existential despair over the unanswered questions of life, then behaves with the emotional maturity of a child half his age. It's parental whiplash. I've toyed with the idea of returning the favor. Look like a mom, talk like an infant, dress like a teen, and act like a toddler. But I think I'll save that for my inevitable decline into dementia . . . or the teen years. At this rate those will probably hit at the same time.

So there you go. A crash course in giftedness. Please note that I am not a gifted expert by any stretch of the imagination, but simply someone who was thrown into the deep end of the gifted pool by giving birth to gifted children. There are many websites and books available to sate your curiosity; some of my favorites can be found in the Resources section, which follows in Appendix B.

Appendix B

Resources

Books

101 Success Secrets for Gifted Kids, by Christine Fonseca.

A Parent's Guide to Gifted Children, by Dr. James Webb, et al.

Emotional Intensity in Gifted Students, by Christine Fonseca.

Making the Choice: When Typical School Doesn't Fit Your Atypical Child, by Corin Barsily Goodwin and Mika Gustavson, MFT.

Misdiagnosis and Dual Diagnoses of Gifted Children and Families, by Dr. James Webb, et al.

Upside-Down Brilliance: The Visual-Spatial Learner, by Dr. Linda Silverman.

Websites

Laughing at Chaos
 www.laughingatchaos.com

Gifted Homeschoolers Forum
 www.giftedhomeschoolers.org

2e Newsletter
 www.2enewsletter.com

Gifted Development Center
 www.gifteddevelopment.com

Gifted Homeschooler Forum: Definitions Page
 www.giftedhomeschoolers.org/definitions.html

Hoagies' Gifted Education Page
 www.hoagiesgifted.com

National Association for Gifted Children
 www.nagc.org

Supporting the Emotional Needs of the Gifted
 www.sengifted.org

About the Author

Jen Merrill is a Chicago-based blogger and writer, having recently returned to her Windy City hometown after 14 years in Denver. After years of jamming her twice-exceptional son into various school settings that didn't quite fit, she's also a new homeschooling mom who couldn't be happier. Well, she could, but that would involve a lengthy vacation with umbrella drinks and nightly turn-down service.

A musician by training and a writer by choice, when she has something to say, Jen says it at her blog, Laughing at Chaos (www.laughingatchaos.com). She loves saving documentaries to her Netflix queue, rolling her own sushi, and pretending she's still as good a flutist as she was back in the day. Her life motto is "If you decide to confide in others, you'll discover you're not alone." Her Walter Mitty fantasy? You're reading it.

16637505R00042

Made in the USA
Lexington, KY
03 August 2012